CROCHET FOR BEGINNERS

A Complete Guide to learn the art of Crochet with All the Tips, Tricks, And Projects Ideas

THEA WEBER

Table of Contents

CHAPTER 5
THE PATTERNS AND PROJECTS. CROCHET PATTERNS

CHAPTER 8

CHAPTER 9

Introduction

A hooked needle is used in the textile craft of crochet to weave and loop together fibers. From handbags & comforters to toys & tea cozies, it's utilized to create a wide variety of products.

Contrary to knitting, its earlier and more traditional cousin, which dates back to the middle ages, crochet, as people recognize it, was created fairly recently, in the early nineteenth century, as a method for creating a less expensive alternative to lace.

Crocheting gradually acquired popularity during the Victorian era, in large part because queen victoria took it up. She is renowned for crocheting eight shawls for South African soldiers. Then, as we entered the twentieth century, crochet was utilized to create complete clothes rather than only decorative items like lace & small accessories like shawls and caps.

However, the 1960s and 1970s were crochet's prime, when items for the home like plant holders & cushion coverings, in addition to clothes like dresses, and tops, including skirts, were especially fashionable. As a growing number of people take up crochet, it appears like the bohemian style of the 1960s and 1970s is undergoing a sort of comeback.

Similar to how knitting stitches may be enlarged, decreased, & combined, crochet stitches may be made in a variety of heights.

Basic swatch for crochet

The stitches, which vary in height & appearance, can be inserted anywhere in your design, unlike basic crochet, that is constructed in stacks such as a straightforward brick wall.

As a consequence, producing super-cool, 3d textured graphics is a reasonably simple artistic expression that one can enjoy while being creative and flexible.

Why enquire about crochet?

Numerous options are easily possible with crochet. Fun is the best justification for learning to crochet. It stimulates your mind and uses your hands in novel ways that are comparable to knitting.

Crochet is incredibly sculptural and may easily carry you in all ways if you picture things in 3 dimensions.

Crochet patterns do well along with cotton yarn, which is considerably lighter to work than wool, so summer artisans will love crocheting in nice weather.

Additionally, crochet is extremely portable because it only takes one hook & always has one continuous stitch, making it ideal for people like you who want to carry your projects with you wherever you go. When the project is in the purse, you don't have to worry about losing more than 100 stitches off the needles.

What is good about crochet?

Mesh trade bags, as well as actual lace doilies, coasters, ornaments, and even lace sweaters, can all be made with crochet.

Given that crochet fabric has the potential to be firmer as that of knit fabric; it is suitable for solid objects like purses in which you want nothing to escape through the threads. Additionally, it has the potential to be more transparent than knitting, making it ideal for lacey tops, shawls, or even curtains.

Because crochet produces cloth more quickly than knitting, it's also perfect for anything you need to make quickly.

When you grab a crochet hook, knitters will indeed be shocked at how quickly your work expands.

Linens, Christmas tree skirts, & baby blankets may all be made easily and satisfactorily rather of being a one-time thing.

The crochet is indeed excellent for little, intricate tasks that require concentration. With a tiny hook & crochet thread, one can make amazingly detailed patterns. Without wasting a lot of money on yarn or knitting heavy items like sweaters, you may love creating beautiful creations.

Saving money is a benefit of crocheting as well. It's going to be a welcome change for knitters using to blow their budget on a couple of skeins of wool because several crochet projects are perfect for cotton or even artificial yarn.

Why crocheting can be difficult?

While crochet movements are quite simple as well as the hook itself guarantees that one can always catch the yarn, a few of the intricacies can be challenging if you haven't mastered the foundations.

Since crochet is similar to bricklaying, where each stitch is made one at the moment and layered on over the previous ones, beginners sometimes struggle with problems about where to place the hook to make each stitch and exactly how to make a brick wall with even sides.

Chapter 1
Basics for crochet

1.1 Easy step by step instructions for crochet

Step 1: How to carry a crochet hook?

Let's get going. Find a cozy workspace with good lighting, and then gather your materials.

KNIFE GRIP

Finding a comfortable technique to handle the yarn & crochet hook is the first stage in this process. The majority of people hold with yarn in the non-dominant hand while holding the hook in the hand that is non-dominant.

The 2 most common methods to grasp a crochet hook are the pencil or a knife.

Pencil grip: place the index and thumb here between the crochet hook as well as the back of your hand. For extra control and balance, use the 3rd finger underneath.

Knife grip: put your hand, palm down, over the hook. Between the index and thumb, grasp the hook. For better control, encircle the crochet hook's shaft with your remaining three fingers.

Holding the yarn for crochet

Spin your yarn thru the fingers of the non-dominant palm to hold it. The yarn should be passed over the pinkie, between your middle & third fingers, and above the index finger. The yarn may be passed underneath the third & middle fingers, over through the index finger, as well as one more time all around the pinky finger to increase tension.

Initially, gripping your yarn in this manner could seem strange, but persist at it. You will eventually discover your preferred method for maintaining pressure on your yarn.

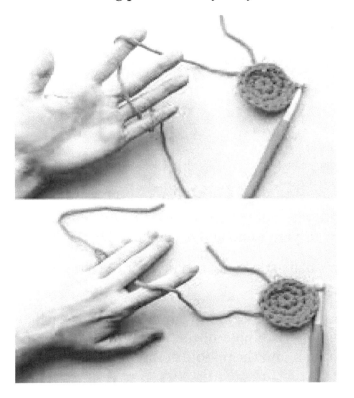

Step 2: How to secure a slip knot?

The yarn should now be tied to your crochet hook with a slip knot.

How to tie a slip knot?

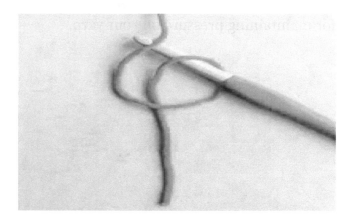

Take some yarn out of the ball. Starting the loop about six inches from your yarn's end and leaving a tail for later weaving in.

The yarn's ball end should be laid over the later part in a clockwise circular motion.

From the front to back, put your crochet hook further into the loop's center. Take hold of the ball end of your yarn with the hook & drag it into the middle of the loop.

To make the loop tighter all around the hook, tighten the yarn at both ends.

Once your slip knot is finished, you can begin crocheting.

Step 3: How to weave over?

Each of the fundamental crochet stitches is created using the "yarn over" technique. For instance, in the following step, you

will produce a beginning chain and, afterward, separate crochet stitches using yarn-overs.

INSTRUCTIONS:

Working yarn is wrapped around the loop in a clockwise motion spanning back to front.

To loop the yarn around the crochet hook, take the left index finger; to rotate the hook beneath the yarn, use the right hand. Both actions have the same results.

You employ the yo motion as one of the fundamental crochet stitches when you've mastered it on its own. Let's move on.

Step 4: How to create a beginning chain?

Making a starting chain is the following step. A starting chain seems to be a collection of chain stitches in crochet that serves as the project's framework.

TO CREATE A BEGINNING CHAIN:

In the right hand, grab the hook, & in the left, the yarn. If your hook isn't already present, place it inside the slip knot.

Between the left hand's thumb & middle finger, grasp the tip of the slip knot.

Alternatively known as "yarn over," slide the working yarn through your hook from rear to front.

To secure the yarn inside the bowl of your hook, twist the hook just a little. Pull the loop of the hook through into the loop. A chain stitch is finished.

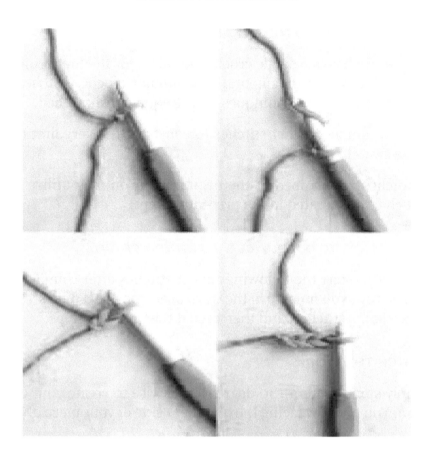

Yarn through the hook, and then pull up an additional loop to create a second chain stitch. Make more and more chain stitches as the pattern specifies by repeating this procedure. Create around eleven chain stitches to replicate my swatch.

Fingers on the left hand should be moved up the chain as one works. Maintain the chain 2 or 3 stitches or more distant from your hook for maximum control.

Please take note that certain patterns will instruct you to flip the chain over & only work the 1st row of your stitches inside the back bar. Your project may have a neater edge if you work through into the rear bar.

Step 5: How to do the single crochet?

Simple stitches like single crochet are ideal for the first project. Among the most fundamental and popular crochet stitches is this one. In crochet techniques, sc is frequently shortened.

Let's use single crochet stitches to construct the very first row of the swatch.

11 stitches are chained at the beginning. (You may utilize the first chain we created in the preceding step.)

Step 6: How to construct the turning chain?

In order to start the following row of stitches after completing the last row, you must turn the work over, construct one or even more chains stitches, and then repeat the previous steps.

SWITCH THE WORK

Simply spin the item 180 degrees clockwise to create your creation. You are now facing the opponent side of your piece of art.

CHAIN ROTATION

One or even more chain stitches must be made once the item has been turned. These chains, referred to as the turning chain,

raise the yarn to the proper height so that the first knot of the following row may be worked.

The length of the stitch you'll be knitting in the following row determines how many chains you need for the turning chain.

Chain one for single crochet.

DOUBLE CROCHET IN HALF: TWO CHAINS

Triple chains in double crochet

Four chains for a triple crochet

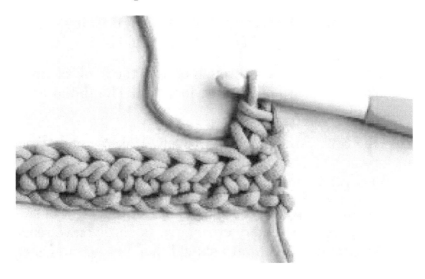

THE TWIST OR THE CHAIN-1, WHICH COMES FIRST?

Which comes first, turning your job or the chain? It doesn't really matter whatever step you complete first.

It is simply important that you choose one approach and stick with it throughout your essay. Additionally, it's a good idea to

rotate your work consistently in either a counterclockwise or clockwise direction.

Step 7: How to perform row 2?

Make the 2nd row of your single crochet knots on the crochet swatch by returning to it. Instead of the initial chain, this row will indeed be crocheted into the single crochet stitches of the preceding row.

Toggle chain 1 as well as the work.

The hook should be inserted between the top two loops of the preceding row's final stitch.

From back to front, re-yarn. Pull up a loop by drawing your yarn through the stitch. On the hook, there should be two loops.

Reverse the yarn & pull it through both of the hook's loops. On the hook, there will only be one loop left. The initial crochet stitch is finished.

Across the row, work from right to left. Make a single crochet loop for each of the 9 remaining stitches by repeating these steps. Verify the number of stitches you have by counting them.

You can now spin your piece to add an additional row of stitches. Continue to add solitary crochet rows once you've reached the length you want. The yarn should then be cut and fastened off.

Step 8: Fastening off

You must fasten off your yarn after completing the final row of the crochet swatch in order to prevent the stitches from unraveling.

To secure off:

Leave a six-inch yarn tail after cutting the yarn.

Bring the yarn tail up through your loop on the hook using the hook.

Pulling on the yarn tail will help to tighten it. Take the crochet hook out of the project.

You could now want to weave the yarn tails in to keep them in place.

Use the yarn tail to thread a souled yarn needle for weaving in the ends. After that, go back & forth across the crocheted fabric with the needle.

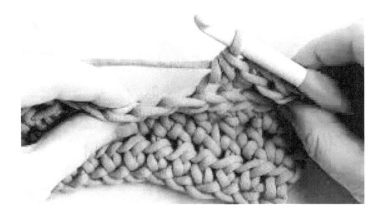

So there you have it. Your initial crocheted swatch is now complete.

1.2 Learning to do half double crochet

One more of the six fundamental crochet stitches is the half-double crochet stitch, sometimes known as hdc. It's a simple, enjoyable stitch for beginners to learn how to make. Baby blankets, cushions, scarves, and cozy sweaters are just a few of the items you may create with half-double crochet.

With one additional yarn-over at the start, each half-double crochet stitch resembles the single crochet stitch. Half-double crochet is longer than a single crochet but shorter than double crochet due to the additional yarn over.

Double crochet technique

The double crochet stitch, also known as dc, is the next stitch in our list of fundamental crochet stitches.

A beginner-friendly stitch, double crochet is used in a variety of patterns, including the traditional granny square pattern.

A double crochet stitch is smaller than just a treble crochet stitch yet taller than either single crochet as well as a half-double stitch. Compared to cloth manufactured from conventional single crochet, dual crochet fabric is a bit more flexible and open.

1.3 Treble crochet techniques

You are capable of learning treble crochet after mastering double crochet.

The pattern notation for triple crochet, also known as treble crochet, is TR.

A treble stitch is higher compared to a dual crochet stitch because it has an additional yarn over. You can increase the number of yarn-overs once you master the fundamental technique to create double-treble & triple-treble stitches.

Treble crochet produces a looser, well-draped cloth. It is frequently utilized in open, airy, and bright patterns.

What is a slip stitch?

Not least among other techniques is indeed the crochet slip stitch. Your shortest of the fundamental crochet stitches is the

slip stitch. Slip stitch is frequently denoted as SL st in patterns.

The slip stitch is a very practical and adaptable method. To slide the yarn throughout a line of stitches without significantly increasing height, use slip stitches. The very last stitch during a round of the crochet can be joined to the beginning stitch of the following round using the slip stitch to create a circle. Last but not least, you might use a top slip stitch to embellish crochet cloth.

1.4 Supplies

Are you interested in knowing what tools you need to begin crocheting? If so, you are in the appropriate place. You can find a detailed list of all the necessary crochet supplies and equipment in this book.

The appropriate tools are crucial if you're just starting to know how to crochet. If you got the necessary high-quality craft supplies & tools, learning will go much more smoothly & be more enjoyable.

It can be challenging to determine which materials you truly need and which ones may be saved for later when you are just starting out with crochet.

1.5 Best crochet materials for beginners

Your crochet hook, as well as the yarn, is the two most crucial crocheting supplies, as you may expect. You can't crochet anything if you don't have these two materials.

You'll also require a yarn needle, one set of scissors, several stitch markers, as well as a measuring tape in the crochet toolkit in combination with the hook as well as yarn.

Let's take a closer look at every one of these crocheting tools and materials.

Crochet hooks

Let's start by discussing the most important tool, which is the crochet hook.

When crocheting, only one hook is used (unlike knitting that requires 2 needles).

You have a wide range of choices while looking for crochet hooks. There are many different types of materials, forms, & sizes of crochet hooks, each with advantages and disadvantages.

Material: a range of materials, including aluminum, steel, and bamboo, plastic and wood are used to make crochet hooks. You'll feel all of these materials in a slightly different way. Metal hooks, for instance, are exceedingly swift & smooth but can be chilly to the touch. On the other hand, plastic hooks might have more "grip" or contact on the yarn despite being lightweight and warm.

Other materials, like bamboo, and resin, including hand-carved wood, are also used to make crochet hooks. If you can, experiment with a few various materials to determine which kind of hook you prefer using.

Shape: there are several distinct forms or styles available for crochet hooks. For instance, boyed brand hooks feature a shorter shaft with a tapered hook head as well as a throat. Hooks from the Susan bates brand have a smaller shaft as well as an inline-style hooked head & throat. To determine your preferred style, it's an excellent idea to try out a few various hooks.

Size: hooks naturally exist in a variety of sizes. The pattern, as well as the yarn you're choosing, will determine the size you require for the upcoming creation. With thin yarns, utilize thin

hooks; with thick yarns, use bigger hooks. Examine the yarn description for a decent place to start if you're unsure about the hook size to use.

Yarn: one of the best elements of beginning a fresh crochet project might be going yarn shopping. But choosing the finest yarn for the upcoming crochet project may feel overwhelming when you're seated in the yarn market and gazing at shelves upon shelves of yarn.

There are numerous different kinds of yarn available for crochet projects. It comes in a broad range of weights, colors, textures, and fiber contents.

Texture: if you're just starting out, it's a good idea to use yarns that are simple to deal with—nothing that's overly fluffy, delicate, smooth, slippery, or rough. As your crocheting skills improve, you might try practicing with fibers that are more delicate or textured.

Color: a wide variety of colors, such as solids, self-striping, & multicolored yarn, are offered in yarn. To make it simpler to notice your stitches, novices should begin with yarns that are lighter in color.

Lace, superfine, fine, dk/light, medium, bulky, super bulky & jumbo is the seven yarn weight classifications. We advise choosing medium-weight or thick yarn when you first start out.

(Remember to adjust the hook size to the type of yarn you select. Examine that crochet hook sizing reference chart or the backside of your yarn package for the recommended hook size.)

Fiber content: yarn is available in both natural & synthetic fibers, including cotton, silk, acrylic, and wool. Since they have a little bit of additional bounce & elasticity than cotton yarns, we suggested practicing with wool or yarns blended with acrylic.

Yarn needle: you'll make use of a yarn needle, which is a sizable, blunt-tipped catheter, to thread in the yarn's ends as well as join sections of crochet. Another name for a yarn needle is a circular knitting spindle or, indeed, a tapestry needle.

Size: the sizes, materials, and styles of yarn needles vary. Depending just on the thickness of the yarn, select the appropriate needle size. For instance, a fabric needle with a wider eye is necessary when dealing with bulky yarn so that you can thread it.

Shape: straight or bent-tip yarn needles are offered. Almost all our crochet projects use straight yarn needles, which we prefer. However, bent-tip yarn syringes are excellent for getting under stitch loops. We believe bent-tip spindles are very helpful for assembling amigurumi parts.

Yarn needles are made of plastic & metal. For practically all crochet tasks, we favor metal yarn needles.

Your best option? Choose from 2 straight & 2 bent-tip steel yarn needles in this value set of 4.

Scissors

Every crochet toolkit needs a decent set of scissors. Your scissors will be used to cut yarn & trim ends.

Any set of razor-sharp scissors will work for crocheting. If you can, we suggest purchasing a compact set of scissors that will fit conveniently in either a project bag or a crochet bag. These stork scissors or yarn snips are really adorable.

Thread markers

You'll need stitch markers, which are little tools, to mark the crochet stitches. Stitch markers may be used to indicate the start of the next round, the completion of one row, or to record decreases and increases.

There are several hues, materials, & shapes available for stitch markers. Select locking or divided ring stitch indicators when crocheting. Avoid purchasing closed stitch markers; they work well for knitting but not for crochet.

You may even manufacture your own stitch marks out of binder clips or hairpin pins if you're on a tight budget.

Tape measures

Necessary crocheting equipment is a tape measure. It will be

used to gauge the crochet work and to determine the width and length of your products.

We advise utilizing a flexible tape measure. It is strong, simple to wrap around objects with three dimensions, and convenient to put in the crochet bag.

1.6 Additional crochet tools and supplies

Once you develop a love for crocheting, you could be inclined to invest in a few additional crocheting supplies and equipment to make the experience even more enjoyable.

Below are a few crocheting "good" tools to take into account.

Hook case for crochet

The best method to arrange and keep your crochet hooks is in a case. Additionally, it's a fantastic way to keep things secure when not in use.

Craft project tote or bag

The best way to transport all of the crochet supplies is in a bag or tote. It's also a perfect location to keep the crochet "work-in-progress" creations.

Knit bowl

You can keep the crochet yarn in a yarn bowl, that is, a porcelain or wooden bowl. It's an excellent method to prevent messy tangling with the yarn balls.

Column counter

To tally the number of rows you've completed, you may use a little tool called a row counter. When dealing with lengthy items like Afghans & blankets, it is very beneficial.

Hook gauge & swatch ruler

We adore using the swatch ruler as well as the hook gauge in tandem to measure the crochet gauge samples. Measure the gauge using the 4-inch square ruler, and utilize the notches to calculate the size of the crochet hook.

Mats and pins for blocking

Crochet creations are blocked using blocking mats & pins. A crochet creation is blocked after shaping & drying to give it the finest appearance possible. Blocking mats & pins may be useful for completing crochet creations that have a polished appearance.

Yarn swift and ball winder

Two tools can be utilized to wrap crochet yarn into balls: a ball winder as well as a yarn swift. To wrap yarn into spheres without tangling it, a yarn swift is useful.

1.7 Abbreviations (us terms)

Hdc – half double crochet

Ch – chain

Ch1sp – the room made by a single chain

Diablo – half double crochet through the back loop only

Sp – space

Dc2tog – double crochet 2 together

Dc – double crochet

St – stitch(s)

Tch – turning chain

Dec – decrease

SK – skip

Ws – Wrong side

Rs – Right side

Chapter 2
All about crochet stitches

Like learning any new skill, learning to crochet requires some time, patience, as well as a few specifically chosen crochet stitches. For making blankets, scarves, shawls, cardigans, as well as other items, here are seven basic crochet stitches. The universe (or crochet) is the oyster once you master them.

2.1 7 Easy crochet stitches for beginners

Are you prepared to begin your own incredible journey with crochet? As we go through each of these basic crochet stitches, we hope you'll join us.

How to do a chain stitch in crochet

Let's begin well with the crochet chain stitch from the very start. Since it's the initial stitch we would use when beginning new crochet designs, it's the most fundamental & the one that novices learn first. The majority of crochet designs begins with a predetermined amount of chain stitches and continues to expand on them throughout the creation.

Pattern shorthand: ch

How to create a starting chain with the chain stitch:

Put together a slip knot.

Enter the slip knot with the crochet hook.

To create a new loop, yarn over & pull through. Your very first chain stitch is here.

Continue until you've reached the required amount of crochet stitches for the foundation chain, and then continue to create the following chain stitch.

If you've never crocheted before, this could seem difficult at first, but with some practice, this simple stitch will seem natural. This is advantageous because different crochet stitch kinds can be joined together using chain stitches.

How to cross one stitch in crochet

It's time to move on to individual crochet stitches when you feel more at ease with the chain stitch. This stitch is quick and simple to construct and is almost as simple as the chain stitch.

It creates a soft texture that complements caps, baby blankets, & scarves perfectly.

Pattern shorthand: sc

Instructions for the single crochet stitch:

Put the hook into the subsequent stitch when you have the starting chain. To make a loop, yarn over again and pull through the yarn. Your hook now has 2 loops on it.

Reverse the yarn and pass it across both loops. One loop of yarn should remain on your hook at the end.

How to crochet double stitches

Once you're familiar well with the sole crochet stitch, move on to this fundamental stitch. The dual crochet stitch is used

frequently in many different crochet patterns & is larger than the sole crochet stitch.

In comparison to the single crochet stitch, it will provide a surface that is more malleable. Additionally, it can be used to make crochet stitches that are more intricate, like the granny stitch.

Dc is a pattern abbreviation.

Details for the double crochet stitch:

Users yarn over before putting the hook into the subsequent stitch, which distinguishes this stitch from the sole crochet stitch.

Yarn over, and then place the hook in the subsequent stitch. Restart your knitting and persevere. On your hook, there will be three loops.

Reverse the yarn & pull it through two loops. On the hook, you'll still have two loops.

Once more, pull via both loops to form a single loop by repeating the process.

How to crochet half-double stitches

Half dual crochet stitches are the following on the list. It resembles a cross in between solitary as well as double crochet stitches and is useful for making blankets, shawls, textured bags, as well as other items.

Hdc is a pattern abbreviation.

Instructions for the half-double crochet stitch:

Yarn over, and then place your hook in the subsequent stitch.

Restart your knitting and persevere. On your hook, there will be two loops.

To create a single loop on the hook, yarn over once more & pull through all the 3 loops.

How to crochet treble stitches

The treble crochet thread will follow. Of all the patterns on this list, one stitch is indeed the tallest (4 chains tall). It requires repetition & builds quickly, producing loose rugs with open, lace-like patterns.

You can add to it and make double treble & triple treble crochet threads after you are comfortable stitching it.

Pattern TR is abbreviated.

Instructions for the treble crochet stitch:

After doubling your yarn, place the hook in the following stitch.

Reverse the yarn & pull it through. On the hook, there will be three loops.

Reverse the yarn & pass it through the initial two loops on your hook.

Over-yarn and pass through the following two loops.

To create a single loop on the hook, continue the procedure one more time, drawing the hook through the final two loops.

Slip stitch crochet stitches: a guide

A simple stitch with numerous applications is the slip stitch. To knit in the round, one method is to slip stitch the very last stitch of a single row to the beginning stitch of the following row.

To transport yarn along a row while raising it, you can also use slip stitches to make flat, invisible stitches. For a neat, finished appearance, you could also include slip stitches to the borders of the crocheted cloth.

Last but not least, crocheted goods can be embellished with slip stitches.

Pattern acronym: SL st

Instructions for the slip stitch in crochet

A slip stitch is just a single crochet stitch that has been simplified.

Put the crochet hook through the following stitch.

Pull your yarn through your stitch as well as the loop over your hook after yarning over.

How to crop out moss stitch stitches

Other names for the moss stitch include the granite, linen, & weaved stitches. Although it appears to be the most complicated

stitch on this ranking, the simple crochet & chain stitches are really only combined in it.

Our textured moss stitch that sits flat but looks amazing along both sides and provides a nice drape, is created by merging these 2 stitches in a simple pattern.

One of the favorite crochet stitches; it can be used to make blankets, shawls, sweaters, headgear, and other items.

Instructions for making moss stitch in crochet:

There should be an appropriate number of chains.

In the fourth chain from the bottom, single crochet (sc).

Single crochet 1, chain (ch) 1, omits next chain (SK).

Repeat: ch 1, skip 1, sc across the row.

Just at the conclusion of the row, turn the project and sc in the space left by chain 1. Across the row, repeat.

Chapter 3
How to crochet with left hand

Right-handed crochet & left-handed crochet are essentially same. Left-handed crocheters hold their hooks in their left hands, while right-handed crocheters hold their yarn.

What you require:

Knitting needle and yarn

Instructions:

Let's begin at the beginning

Always keep in mind that practice makes perfect

3.1 Holding your crochet hook when crocheting

With your hook pointed backwards toward the thumbnail, secure it in place between the dominant hand's fingers and thumb. This hold should be pleasant yet firm. As you get more at ease, you'll discover that the hook will establish its very own comfort level.

3.2 Crochet techniques: holding your yarn

When crocheting, maintaining the even pressure upon that yarn is essential for getting even stitches. This really is especially crucial if you're designing sizing-specific patterns, like clothing. The operating loop is shown in this image being gripped between the right hand's thumb & middle finger & wrapping

over the forefinger to adjust tension. To aid in maintaining tension and preventing tangling, lace your yarn using the other fingers. Once more, you'll discover a comfort zone while you work. Nothing obligates you to carry it out exactly this way.

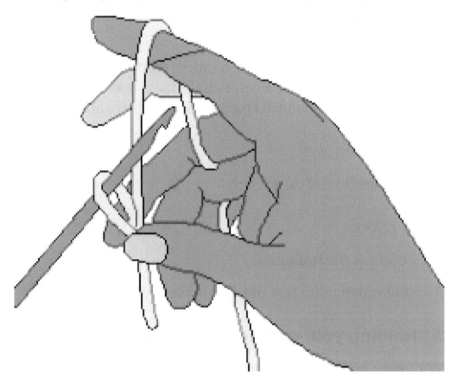

3.3 Beginning loop: crochet instructions

The first stitch used is a slip knot. In order to work, we normally push the hook through the entire operating loop in the other direction, spin, and yarn over, then draw the hook through to the loop. Many prefer to manually tie a knot before inserting the hook to start functioning.

Yarn over, a crochet technique

Shorthand: yo

Yarn over simply refers to the act of wrapping the yarn around the needle from the front to back in order to catch it and allow it to be drawn through into the loop.

3.4 Chain stitch: a crochet technique

Shorthand: ch

The bottom row & rings are created using the most fundamental stitch, the chain stitch. To create a stitch, one merely yarn over again & pull through to the loop. It's all about tension management, which is sometimes easier said than done. Repeat this till you're able to create a chain of uniform-looking loops.

How to make a ring in crochet

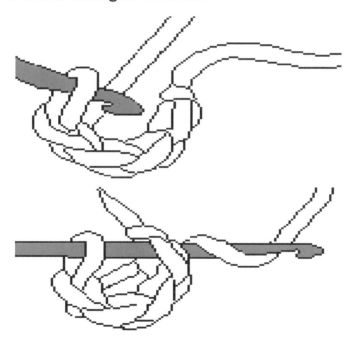

A desired amount of chain stitches are joined end to end to form a ring. Chain as many times as necessary, then thread the hook into the first stitch. Wrap the yarn through the 2 loops on the needle and re-yarn. Rings may be used as embellishments, like as the popcorn stitch, or to start blocks like granny squares.

3.5 Single crocheting instructions

The sc abbreviation

The act of taking up a loop and loops out of a preceding stitch is referred to as crocheting. You'll yarn again & pull through your loops once, as indicated by the term "single." despite the fact that it doesn't look particularly appealing, this stitch has the ability to create entire products. Pick up both the front & back strands from the required stitch (typically the one after it, unless otherwise stated), yarn over, & drag through your loop to complete a single crochet.

3.6 Crocheting technique: double crochet

Diacritical marks: dc

You yarn across; take up the appropriate stitch's front loop in this case. Pull the yarn around the initial of the hook's 3 loops after reversing it. Reverse the yarn and pass it through the final 2 loops over the hook. Dc in every thread for a dense weave; almost every stitch for a softer weave.

3.7 Crocheting technique: half-double crochet

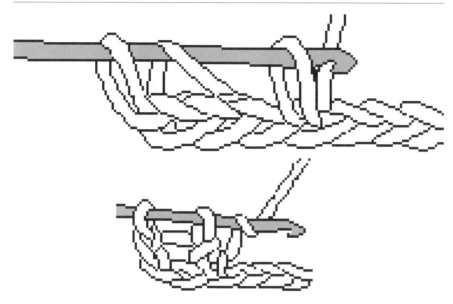

Shorthand: HD

Similar to a double crochet, you start by yarning over before picking up its initial loop of your required stitch. Reverse the yarn and pass it through each three of the hook's loops. Every stitch should be HD for a tight texture; just about every stitch should be HD for a loose weave.

3.8 Crochet technique: triple crochet

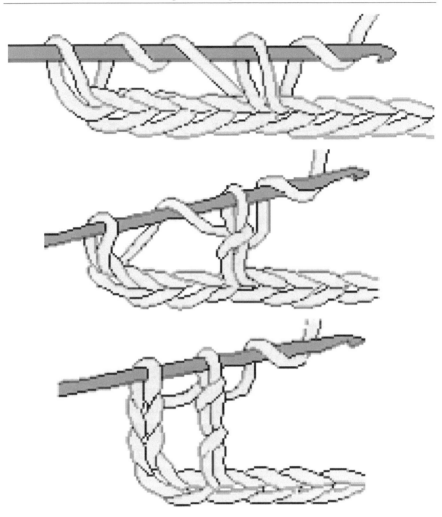

The letters: Tc

After yarning over twice, take up at front loop of your desired stitch to start the triple crochet. Reverse the yarn & thread it across the hook's first 2 loops. Continue doing this till the chain is free of all loops. Single stitch should be Tc for a tight weave; almost every stitch should be used for for a loose weave.

3.9 Tying off: a crochet technique

Add an additional chain stitch, trim the end, & draw the chain all the way across the loop. To tie the end, pull gently on it.

Chapter 4

Crochet hints and tips hints for crochet beginners

4.1 Make sure your stitches are loose and loosened

It's completely normal to have tension while you practice something new. Your tendency will be to hold the hook more tightly as the stitch one learns more complex. Resist the desire, breathe in deeply and maintain loose, relaxed stitches. Your ability to enter your hook will be simpler, and the method will be quicker the tighter the stitches are.

4.2 Rehearse, rehearse, and rehearse

Before beginning, understand the pattern you wish to create. Grab the hook & yarn and practice a couple of the stitches listed if you haven't attempted them before (double crochet, single crochet, shell stitches, for example). By the time you arrive at that stitch inside the design, you'll be completely at ease with doing the stitch.

Pro tip: the majority of designs advice creating a "gauge swatch," which is often a square swatch measuring 4 by 4 inches. As you make the gauge swatch, practice your fresh stitches to polish your technique and ensure that you're making the product to the right size.

4.3 Examine various tools

It can be beneficial to invest in some different hooks to test out if you're just looking to start. You could require bait with a wider bowl or mouth if you're having trouble catching the loop on it. You may require a hook along with a pointier head if you're having trouble getting the hook into your stitch. The distinction could be all in the hook.

4.4 Examine various yarns.

Beginners usually do best with smooth, worsted-weight yarn, which doesn't split easily. However, each individual has a different taste. Please feel free to experiment with the many yarns we have available.

4.5 Get to know gauge

Avoid making this classic rookie error. Gauge is crucial. Gauge informs you of the number of stitches & rows that should fit into a specific number of inches. This should be included in every pattern. You must match the gauge to the measurements specified in the pattern if you desire your finished product to look exactly like the examples you've seen or to fit a specific size. Many individuals omit this step, as well as occasionally; they wind up with hats that are big enough to serve as chair covers. Early gauge education will pay dividends in the long run.

4.6 Whether to frog or choose not to frog is up to you

Describe frogging. It might be worthwhile to go back and correct a mistake if you pay attention to every detail and notice one a few rows back. Make a decision regarding whether you desire to go back as well as rectify the error if it is not obvious. Each person has a unique preference. Don't feel bad about what you choose.

4.7 Be gentle with yourself

Mistakes do occur. Crocheters of all skill levels and attention to detail make silly mistakes in their craft. Nobody's first project is flawless. Don't punish yourself for errors. Take pride in your newfound knowledge, and remember that you will get better with practice.

4.8 Before beginning to crochet, convert skeins into balls of yarn.

You could be tempted to pull the name off the yarn skein and start working if you're eager to get the project going. Theoretically, you may crochet with yarn skeins, but in numerous instances, winding the skein together into a ball first would yield better results. For beginners, this is particularly true.

Compared to skeins, yarn balls have the following advantages:

Prevent tangling. In conclusion, yarn skeins with a center pull may easily tangle. Yarn balls have a lower chance of tangling.

Increase in tension. Try using a yarn ball instead of a strand if you have trouble getting even tension.

Although ball winders seem to be available to assist you, you may alternatively complete the task by hand.

4.9 Remove barriers before crocheting

Long hair: comb as well as tie backs your hair if it is long sufficient to get in the way before you begin crocheting. This helps you keep your hair out of your job.

Remove any jewelry before beginning to crochet, particularly rings and bracelets. Yarn can tangle with jewelry and prevent you from progressing.

Keep animals away from the room when crocheting, if at all feasible. A spinning ball of yarn seems to be irresistible to cats. A cat can easily sabotage a crocheted item as well.

4.10 Properly position the yarn

As you crochet, place the yarn ball so that it may unravel easily.

You may place the yarn ball in your lap or at the feet if you're crocheting at your house in a cozy chair, according to your preference.

Put the yarn ball within a tote bag if you're crocheting while flying or driving to prevent it from sliding about and unraveling.

4.11 Change your crochet hooks as necessary

Beginner crocheters frequently work too closely or too loosely.

Select a bigger crochet hook if the work is too tight.

A small crochet hook should be used if the work is too loose.

Remember that your hook size listed on the yarn label is only intended as a suggestion.

Before beginning a project, practice using hooks. When you're creating the gauge swatches seems to be the optimum time to accomplish this.

4.12 Steer clear of switching hooks mid-project.

All throughout your project, your stitches should be the same. You run the danger of introducing inconsistencies if you change hooks. Problems could arise even with size changes from one manufacturer's hook to another's.

Manufacturers don't always use the same hook size.

You might need to hold the hook differently or form your stitches differently due to little variations in hook shaping.

4.13 Use ergonomically designed crochet hooks

Crochet hooks with ergonomic designs are made to be cozy. If you can locate an ergonomic hook that you like, it might make crocheting time more delightful than it otherwise would be.

4.14 Spend some time creating gauge swatches

You might feel inclined to believe making crocheting gauge swatches is a time-consuming endeavor. It's probably the most important aspect of the project, especially if it's a garment. The project is most likely to be the incorrect size if one omits the gauge swatch.

15. Be bold and unafraid

Pull out your stitches until that point & start again if you discover an error some rows back.

4.16 Don't be hesitant to try new things

There's no "crochet police," and if your experiment fails, nothing negative will occur to you. The two most effective approaches to moving past the novice stage are practice and experimentation. Think about some straightforward tests:

1. Change the hues in a pattern

2. Pick several yarns

3. Add or remove information: if a design asks for fringe that you don't like, use an edging instead, or decorate a simple hat with flowers.

4. Don't be hesitant to try more challenging tests as you gain knowledge:

5. Add patterns to a simple design.

6. Use different types of stitching.

7. Make improvements to the customizations: give a sweater long sleeves rather than short sleeves and change the collar.

8. Even though some of these trials might not be successful, you will learn something new from each one.

4.17 Make companions who crochet

You've undoubtedly worked out by this point that there're numerous viable methods for crocheting. Every experienced crocheter has a different set of insights and knowledge to offer.

4.18 Magic ring

The majority of crochet designs which are worked in rounds begin with a magic ring, if not all of them.

It is a different method for making a ring than chaining as well as slip-stitching into the initial chain.

A chain and slip stitch leaves a gap in the center of the project, whereas a magic ring entirely seals it.

Two procedures exist for making a magic ring:

Variant 1

Making a knot with the yarn from the commencement and crossing the end beneath the yarn going from the end.

With your fingertips, hold the area where the yarns converge.

Allow the skein of yarn to trail behind the loop before slipping the hook beneath it and across to capture the edge of your loop that is furthest from the hook.

Pull the loop all the way up to the rings top.

Hold your loop as you do so. Release the area where the multiple threads converge.

Chain 1 and finish your stitch if you're working on a single crochet item. Chain 2 if you are using double crochet for your project.

In your ring, crochet several stitches in accordance with your pattern.

Variant 2

The yarn should form an "x" on your fingers after being twice wrapped over two of the fingers.

Go over the primary string and underneath the second one with your hook, twist, as well as pull through.

Start off by making just several chains in your ring.

4.19 Connecting yarn together (once one skein is finished and a new one is being started)

Knowing how to properly join two strands together is crucial when working on a lengthy project that calls for several skeins of yarn.

It is possible to tie it in a knot, but there is no assurance that they won't untie it.

Additionally, it leaves off two tiny tails that might be challenging to include in your creation.

You are making a transition that is more seamless by using a magic knot.

This is how:

The yarn you are using right now should have around 3 inches left after you finish crocheting.

At that time, hold the new yarn beside the old yarn while trimming the new yarn's tail to roughly three inches.

Holding the two yarns together, crochet one stitch. Release the old yarn, & start crocheting well with a new one.

This technique is a guaranteed way to prevent the yarns from splitting and prevents your item from getting bumps & knots all over it.

4.20 Alternating colors

You'll probably begin to switch colors while crocheting as you advance to more challenging designs.

For a nice, clean appearance to the project, you should smoothly transition between the different shades when working with yarn which is not self-striping to create a stripe design or while working on a color block project.

This is how:

Start making a standard crochet stitch well with yarn you're using right already when you stop crocheting. Hook it in, yarn it over, lift up a loop, and stop.

Place the brand-new yarn on your hook & hold the tail between your fingers to complete the stitch. Continually crochet using the new yarn.

This is indeed a quick and easy way to change the color of yarn.

4.21 Foundation chain without chain

The very first line of chains & the inaugural row of stitches is referred to as chainless chains in crochet.

In general, this method makes crocheting simpler. The initial row of regular stitches is prevented from twisting as they would otherwise.

Since you work the base chains as well as the initial row of stitches together, it also avoids the frustration of realizing you forgot to count the chains on the bottom row.

A foundation chain is made as follows:

Make a slip-knot & chain two.

The hook should be inserted into the initial chain to capture the left of the chain as well as the middle of the stitch.

Make a loop with yarn & draw it up. Your hook ought to have two loops.

Reverse the yarn & create a new loop.

Reverse the yarn and put the hook via both loops. The very first single crochet was made by you.

Repeat the first stage of the stitching procedure by putting the hook further into the chain of the preceding stitch.

Work the single crochets like before, but this time works them sideways. Compared to attempting to do it horizontally, it will be simpler.

You've now acquired a new crochet skill and saved yourself some time.

4.22 Over-crocheting ends

The worst part of crocheting is weaving ends in.

It is tiresome & takes a long time. Fortunately, there is an alternative to weaving or clipping those endings to keep them in.

When you've finished cutting your yarn, bring the end up to the row you're working on and crochet across it until it vanishes.

By doing this, you avoid having to painfully weave them in and get those out of the way.

4.23 Change the size of the hook for the lead to the formation.

Many novices struggle to maintain consistent pressure on your foundation chain. One may create an even chain through practice; you'll be able to fix it by switching the chain's hook.

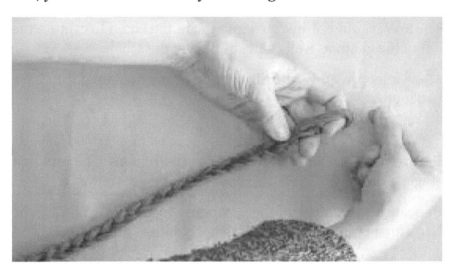

Move up a hook size if you notice that the starting chain seems significantly tighter than the remainder of the piece and is pulling inward. Move down your hook size if such foundation chain becomes too loose & sitting broader than the piece.

4.24 Count the stitches to create even, straight edges.

If you've ever noticed that your piece seemed to get thinner or broader as one is working on it, the thread count is likely off. As you proceed to the following row, you could unintentionally miss spaces or include stitches to the end. There are several solutions to this. To ensure you don't skip any spaces, you may pinch your fabric between the fingers, placing your thumb at every stitch, and afterward move the fingers across the row as one go. The initial and final stitches of each row may also be marked using a stitch marker. Put the marking as when you've finished working on that area so you won't forget to do so.

You might also just count. If you began having 10 sc and therefore only got to 9 at the finish of the row, you skipped one and could go back and rectify it.

4.25 To measure stitches, look at the vs.

Looking at the vs. is a quick and simple technique to count stitches. Similar to the beginning chain, the ends of the stitches form a v.

Put the hook mostly under loops of your v while you weave into a thread. Therefore, to determine how many stitches that have, measure the vs. on the top rather than the underlying stitches.

4.26 Apply invisible reductions

The best technique to decline in sc is with invisible decreases. We recently discovered a crochet tip, and even though we still adore using our traditional decrease, now this is much more co-vert. Insert the hook into the front looping of the next 2 places, yarn over, pull across both loops, and yarn over to complete the sc. This creates an unseen decrease.

4.27 Instead of a connected chain, use the magic loop.

Use your magic loop when starting from the center to construct a ring rather than making a chain, as well as slip sewing a ring together. A magic loop allows you to begin a loop of every size and is simpler to expand than a small ch-3 loop. To ensure that there isn't a tiny hole left open, you may also pull your loop closed tightly.

In comparison to a linked chain, they produce better quality and are simply far more adaptable.

4.28 Utilize stitch markers

Many of the more experienced crocheters may believe you may skip this step because stitch markers are mentioned in every guide for beginning crocheters. Nope.

Stitch markers seem to be really useful and simplify your life. To avoid having to measure every stitch to determine if the round is complete, you may use them to indicate the very first gap in the round. Use them to indicate rows in order to go back and count the number you've completed. Then, if you make an error, you'll know if the numbers are incorrect instead of waiting for 5 rows to find out. You may use them to divide pattern repeats. Well, before we link our amigurumi pieces connected, we use our stitch markers to keep the pieces together so we can observe how it's progressing.

4.29 Space out round increases for rounded circles

Do the circles frequently resemble hexagons? It is so that they can create points since a stand expansion pattern often stacks the boosts at the same distance. Your genuine increases just stack on the base of each other as one increase the distance between increases. As a result, the hexagon shape is enhanced.

Sc 4, raise, repeat to the conclusion of the round.

Sc 5, rise, repeat to the conclusion of the round.

Stagger the increases to correct this. It resembles the outer circular having just been rotated. Before your initial rise in the following round, only work a portion of the sc; after that, continue all around the pattern, finishing with the entire sc. In this manner, all you're doing is moving the increases spaces.

Phase 8: sc 3, increase; repeat from *sc 6, increase* to the last 3; sc 3.

Just anytime it seems too hexagonal, you don't have to do it for each round.

4.30 Record rows as one complete them.

Establish the habit of noting them on the pattern to maintain track if you frequently lose track of where you're at in a design or the number of rows you've done. After working the pattern,

put it out with a simple cross next to the row no. Or choose to underline the row. Whatever enables you to realize that it has been completed?

Use simple calculations in the pattern's borders or on a post-it note for designs that ask users to work a certain number of rows or increase every nth row. We record the first row or round with a stitch marker, and afterward, we keep track of the remainder with my tallies. In this manner, it is simple for me to maintain my position in the pattern even if we move away from it, as well as easy simple for me to double-check.

Chapter 5

The patterns and projects. Crochet patterns for beginners

5.1 Golden twist headband

You will require:

Crochet hook size h

Scissors

Needle to kit in ends

You could definitely simply single crochet this whole headband if you're a complete beginner. You'll get a similar look. Using chain 15 & single crochet, work each row till the piece is the proper length to fit the head comfortably.

For this design, you must be able to single crochet & chain stitch.

You are basically making a large, long rectangle out of crocheting that you'll twist and sew together afterward.

The basic chain is there. Your headband will be this wide. You'll now continue to follow the crochet design until you get the desired length for your head.

The reversible nature of the cloth makes it ideal for this "twist" headband. Simply fold it in half as shown.

Pattern:

Chain 15

Single crochet across row one, chain one, turn

Loop from * to *, sc in the last stitch, chain 1, turn. Row 2: sc in the initial stitch, *ch 1, SK st, sc in the next stitch*

Sc in the first stitch of row three, *ch 1, SK stitch, sc in the next chain stitch, continue from * to *, sc in the last stitch, chain 1, flip.

Duplicate row 3 until the piece is 21 inches long or wide enough to wrap loosely around the head.

You'll single crochet over the whole piece when the piece attains the preferred length.

Assembly

Twist the large rectangular piece once & join the ends while holding it. With the preferred method, stitched ends. A whip stitch will do. Integrate your ends.

5.2 Flower girl cottage

Simple snowflake crochet pattern

G hook is advised, or use your preferred hook size.

Little pieces of preferred yarn or cotton

Utilize the magic circle method for closed centers.

Or

Chain 5

Slip stitch into the first chain to create a circle.

Round 1:

Ch 4 (which works as hdc, ch 2, and so on), then work it into the magic circle five times.

Round 2:

Fill the six spaces that were just made with work.

SL st in the first empty place towards the left of the hook to start.

The first group of snowflakes

Ch3, SL st in the same location

Ch 5, SL st in the identical location

Ch 3, SL st in the identical location

Follow these steps to complete the remaining clusters: *ch 1, SL st into the following area, ch 3, SL st, ch 5, SL st, ch 3, SL st*

Four more times between * and *.

Ch 1, slips stitch into the initial stitch of this round, & bind off.

5.3 Beautiful crochet scarf pattern for beginners

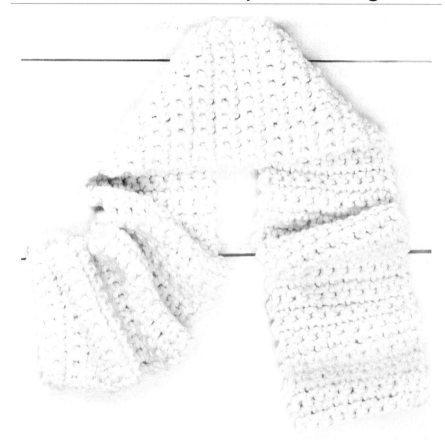

Materials

Just under 196 yards or two skeins of wool-ease heavy & quick or another ultra-bulky six yarn

9 mm crochet hook

Scissors

Tape measure

Crochet needle

Chain (ch) stitch:

A basic crochet stitch is frequently the starting point for other stitches that are added to projects.

Put your slip knot in it.

The hook should be inserted through the slip knot side first. Yarn should be brought over the hook's shaft from rear to front & caught with the hook's throat.

Hook the yarn by pulling it through the slip knot. One chain stitch will be created by this action.

Till you get the required amount of stitches for such a pattern, repeat steps 2 and 3 as necessary. The hook will still have one loop.

Abbreviations for crochet

Chain stitch = (ch)

Single crochet = (sc)

"Stitch" (es) = st(s)

Size

Approximately 6.5" wide by 65" long when finished

Gauge

Gauge: 7 sc x 4 rows equals 4 by 6 inches.

Gauge design:

Ch 8 and proceed for 4 rows as directed by the pattern.

Notes

Written in American English

Use the scarf size guide, crochet more rows to produce a longer, broader scarf, or begin with a larger foundation chain.

If necessary, you may obtain the gauge using a larger or smaller hook.

To create an infinity scarf out of crochet, connect the 2 ends of a scarf together.

The first steps of a scarf pattern

Foundation row: ch 11 with extremely bulky yarn.

Row 1: sc once in each ch across to start the very next row, starting with the second chain from the hook (10)

Row 2: sc once in each stitch across the row, beginning with the first stitch (not ch 1). (10)

Repeat row 2 to complete rows 3-101. (10)

Repeat row 2 to complete rows 3-101. (10)

To complete the scarf, cut the yarn following row 101 (the last row), then use a yarn hook to weave any loose ends into the fabric of the scarf.

5.4 Easy beginner crochet washcloth pattern

Materials

Size J 6 mm crochet hook

Premier Home Yarn less than 40 yards or any four weight cotton or cotton blend yarn

Yarn needle

Scissors

Completed size

An about 6' × 6' square

Notes

Every simple crochet pattern is written using common us terminology.

This washcloth design can be made with any gauge.

Link any even quantity of times to alter the length of these washcloths.

The formula

Ch 26

Row 1: sc into the second chain from the hook and into each subsequent chain across. Turn. (25)

Row 2: ch 1, in the initial stitch, work 1 hdc, then work 1 sc into the following stitch. Repeat from * all over the row, finishing with one hdc in the final stitch.

Row 3: ch 1, sc in each stitch across, turning when each stitch is completed.

Replicate rows 2 and 3 from row 4 to row 27.

Finishing: tie off, and then use a yarn needle to weave in any loose ends.

5.5 Crocheted washcloth set

Materials:

Size of hook(s): 5.5 mm

Weight of yarn: worsted

Cotton is the favorite choice of yarn.

Shades dusty rose & navy from universal cotton ultimate are recommended yarns.

Yardage of yarn: 65 yards

Tools: tapestry needle, scissors

Dimensions when finished: 9.5" by 9.5"

2 inches equals 5.5 single crochets.

Details of the pattern: two dishcloths were made in the example using the colors provided.

Special remarks:

Sc stands for single crochet, st for stitch, and dc stands for double crochet.

The style

Ch 26

Row 1: sc in each stitch across and through the second chain from your hook.

Sc through each stitch across row 2 after ch 1 turns.

Ch1, turn in row three. Sc into the initial 2 stitches. * continue from * through, sc into the initial stitch, then dc into the next. Sc through into the final 3 stitches.

Ch1, turn in row four. Sc further into the initial stitch. Continue from * across, sc in the first stitch, and dc into the next one. Sc through into the final two stitches.

Continue rows three and four from rows 5-29.

Ch1, turn, and sc into each stitch across rows 30-31.

Cut the yarn, tie it off, and weave the ends in.

5.6 Reusable body scrubbers made of crochet

Size / finished dimensions

Between two and three inches in diameter

Gauge

This pattern does not require a specific gauge. Attempt a larger hook if you're having difficulties getting the stitches on it; if they keep slipping off, try a shorter hook.

Abbreviations

Chain stitch= ch

is the required number of stitches, and ch # equals chain # stitches.

The space created by the stated amount of the chain stitches inside the preceding row or round is known as a "ch-# Sp" or "chain-# space."

Half double crochet, or hdc

Rp = repeat

Round = rnd(s) (s)

Single crochet (sc)

SL = slip

Space is sp.

The word "stitch" (es)

Repeat the directives in the brackets as necessary

Notes

American crochet terminology is used throughout the directions. Beginning with such a ring, each scrubby is stitched in the round.

What you'll require:

Resources / tools

5.0 mm us h/8 crochet hook

Tapestry needle or yarn

Scissors

Materials:

Cotton yarn of worsted weight, 8 to 10 yards.

Instructions:

Create a ring

Slip knot, then chain 4. SL st together to make a ring.

Framework round

Round 1: join with a SL st to the first ch after [ch 1, sc through into ring] six times.

We recommend 12 stitches.

Rounds of half double crochet are increased.

To expand, add 2 half double crochet stitches through every chain space beneath the first chain of the previous round.

Round two: ch 2, [two hdc through to the next ch-1 gap, ch 1] six times; link with a SL st to the first Ch.

There need to be 18 stitches.

Round increase in single crochet

Round 3: ch two, [sc 2, ch 1] 9 times; join by sewing to the first stitch.

There need to be 27 stitches.

Edging in picots

Rnd 4 is as follows: ch 1, [ch 3, SL st during next stitch, sc during next stitch] 13 repeats, ch 3, and SL st during the last stitch.

Cut yarn, retaining a 4-inch tail, and fasten off. Utilizing a string or weaving needle, weave the ends in.

Utilize your completed face scrubby.

These quick-to-finish rounds are pleasant to work on. They're indeed a fantastic way to finish off skeins after making dishcloths. Create a large number of scrubbies so that you have several on hand. Use them to remove makeup or as little washcloths to wipe the face in the morning.

The used scrubbies should be gathered in a mesh washing bag and washed before use.

These then make wonderful presents. Create scrubbies in a single color or a spectrum of colors. Create a homemade mini-spa gift by combining them with such a good soap bar.

5.7 Work a pretty heart in crochet

What you'll require:

Resources / tools

Use a crochet hook that is the same size as the yarn.

Tapestry needle or yarn

Materials

4 yards of yarn

Instructions:

With a ring, begin the crocheted heart.

Create the foundational ring on which the crochet will be built first. To create a ring, tie a slip knot, chain 4, & slip stitch together. Turn your project around, so the slipped knot is located in the back.

Do single crochet threads during round one.

Single crochet ten times into the center of the ring after chaining 1 for the twisting chain. Slip stitch in addition to the sliding stitch you used to create the ring. Normally, you should join to the rotating chain, but by moving the join, you can better form the cross indent. All around the circle, there should be 11 stitches.

Work dual & half double crochet threads in round two.

Only double crochet into the initial single crochet starting round one, skipping the turning chain.

2 times in the double crocheted chain stitch 1.

Two times in the partial double crochet thread. Twice [dc, ch 1]. Twice [hdc, ch 1].

Chain double crochet stitch 1.

Twice in the partial double chain stitch 1.

Two times in double crocheting chain stitch 1.

In the final 2 stitches, slip stitch.

There should be 19 stitches all the way all around the circle that is beginning to resemble a heart.

Work solitary crochet stitches round in three.

For a rotating chain, chain one. Eight repetitions in one crochet thread 1. On round 2, insert the solitary crochets into chain stitch spaces rather than the open spaces. Before the first double crochet stitch, single hook 2 through into chain. 9 chains of one single crochet hook. In the final stitch, slip stitch.

Complete the crocheted heart

After cutting, leave around 6 inches of yarn. Using a thread or tapestry needle, tighten the final stitch & thread the ends in. The sweetheart shape is completed by weaving the hook towards the heart indent while you fasten the yarn there.

5.8 Make a baby blanket out of crocheted material

What you'll require:

Resources / tools

Crochet needle

Tatting needle

Sticky note

Materials

Baby yarn by bernat

Sizes of blankets: preemie, newborn, and toddler

Preemie, infant, & toddler sizes are all covered by the directions in just this crocheted baby blanket pattern. The lowest size is listed initially in the instructions, and adjustments for the bigger sizes are given in parenthesis.

If you want to include a baby blanket border, your completed blanket will be slightly larger than the measurements provided here because they do not include any edging.

The tiniest blanket is for preemies and is around 26 inches broad by 34 inches in length. Based on how tightly you crochet, one will need 2 to 3 5-oz strands of bernat softie yarn to finish this creation. You'll require about 724 yards (662 meters) of yarn for your blanket itself and a little bit extra for the gauge swatch.

Blanket for a newborn or recipient: the medium-sized comforter is 30 inches wide. If you like a blanket that is more rectangular in shape, you can extend it a little lengthier. In such a case, strive for 30" by 34". Based on how tightly you crochet, you'll require 2 to 3 of the 5-oz skeins of bernat softie with this size.

Toddler: the biggest blanket is 36 inches x 44 inches in size. To crochet this length, you'll need 4 5-oz skeins of bernat softie.

Symbols for abbreviations in this pattern

The chain is Ch.

The space created when one crochets one chain stitch inside the row before is known as a "ch-1 Sp," or "chain 1 space."

Rp = repeat

Single crochet (sc)

Stitch

Gauge

While crocheting your stitch pattern, as shown below, the stitch gauge is 4 stitches per inch.

Row gauge: for this design, your row gauge is just not crucial.

Baby blanket crochet instructions

Start row one

Ch 105 (121, 145). (121, 145). Keep in mind that the directions are for the little size.

The very first ch above your hook should have a stitch marking in it. 3rd chain from hook: sc. [ch 1, skip a next ch, sc in the next Ch.] Repeat all the way down the row. Ch1, turn.

Begin on row two

[Ch 1] sc in the following ch-1 sp. Repeat the bracketed sequence throughout the remaining rows. Work a sc stitch into the stitch where the marker was at the finish of the row; you can take out the label before sewing the stitch. Ch1, turn.

Continue with rows 3 and up

All subsequent rows are identical to row 2, with the exception of one small modification: at the conclusion of each row, work your final slip stitch into the twisting chain of the row before. Replicate this row up to the required length for the baby blanket.

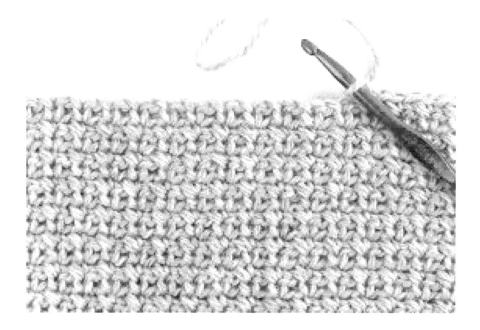

Finish the blanket.

Cut your yarn whenever the baby blanket reaches the desired length, leaving a minimum of 6 inches of additional yarn. Use the rope end to loop the tapestry needle, and then thread the yarn's loose thread into the blanket. Continue with any additional dangling threads on the bedspread.

You don't need any extra edging for this crochet design; however, if you do, you may add one. There are numerous options for baby blanket edgings. The blanket's edge can be finished with a straightforward single crochet technique that complements the sample's single crochet motif.

Chapter 6
Types of crochet

6.1 Amigurumi crochet

The creation of tiny, stuffed toys and creatures out of crocheted or knitted yarn is known as this crochet art form, which has its roots in japan. Nuigurumi is a stuffed animal, whereas ami means knitting or crochet. Amigurumi is when a small doll/ toy is fashioned entirely out of yarn. Subjects for amigurumi that are popular include Mario kart, plants vs. Zombies, & hello kitty.

Things you can create with amigurumi crochet

- Playthings for kids
- Bigger novelty pillows and home goods
- Fan gear

6.2 Aran crochet

Refers to crochet that is ribbed or cabled. Chunky beanies, jackets, and scarves may all be made with this crochet technique, which is generally done in a celtic style by interlocking cables. When you see the word "Aran" in a pattern, keep in mind that it can also refer to a certain amount of yarn.

Things you can do with Aran crochet

- Coverlets
- Scarves

- Lapgans
- Coats
- Jackets

6.3 German crocheting

This is a traditional crochet stitch which is worked in rounds, much like granny squares. Instead of a harsh change in color, such as with granny squares, it enables subtle color changes and produces a thick fabric. Each portion is handled in two stages: a row of groups at the bottom, followed by a row of casings at the top. Bavarian crochet resembles extremely ornate granny squares.

Things you can make with Bavarian crochet

- Coverlets

The shawls

6.4 Crochet from Bosnia

Only such crochet slip thread worked in various locations of a needle from the previous row is used in Bosnian crochet to create a dense, knit-like fabric. Bosnian crochet hooks are available to purchase; however, normal crochet hooks may also be used. Another name for it is shepherd's knitting. Additionally, it resembles crocheting a lot. It's not a particularly trendy style right now; therefore, if you come across it, you might assume it's crocheted.

Things you can make with Bosnian crochet

* Shawls

The beanies

* Smaller stuff because it takes a lot of time.

6.5 Crochet bullion

This is really a particular crochet stitch made by wrapping yarn around an extremely long hook several times to create a recognizable & distinctive "roll" stitch. Bullion crochet can typically utilize patterns as opposed to programs based on fabric. It produces work with a thick, uniform, spherical pattern.

* Stiff objects, such as placemats
* Decorational motifs

6.6 Crochet broomstick

The stitches are constructed around a wide and long, like something of a broomstick handle, and are a historical crochet stitch which is also frequently referred to as jiffy lace. These days, the majority of crocheters who make broomstick lace use enormous crochet hooks as well as thick dowels. Broomstick lace seems to be a fantastic crochet technique to learn, and the finished product is stunning and distinctive.

Things you can create with broomstick crochet

- Beautiful shawls
- throw blankets used as ornamentation

6.7 Crochet in Bruges

This technique is applied to manufacture Bruges lace, wherein elaborate lace designs are formed by creating crochet "ribbons" but then crocheting them together. Most grandmothers have some handmade crocheted things in the Bruges style stashed away in cabinets and protected with acid-free paper.

- Complex shawls
- clothes embellishments
- Tablecloths

6.8 Crochet on a clothesline

In order to create circular mats & baskets that maintain their shape, classic crochet stitches have been done over a piece of rope or a length of strong twine resembling a clothesline. This can be dated directly to artisans in Africa & Nepal, where it is frequently viewed as an experimental technique.

Things you can make with the clothesline crochet style

- Bundles
- Mats
- hanging structures for walls

6.9 Lace crochet clones

This type of crochet was developed because it was quicker and simpler to make than needlepoint lace, and it has strong ties to Irish lace crochet. The clone's crochet skill set includes the clones knot. Clones lace is a very useful crochet pattern that was employed for military objectives.

Things you can do with clones lace crochet

- Open-ended neck scarves
- Feminine shirts and dresses

6.10 Crochet with a hook

To generate double-sided crocheted, cro-hook crochet is performed using a double-ended hook. It enables your crocheter to weave stitches onto or off the opposite end of their item without worrying about whether something is right side up or wrong. Cro-knit is another name for this. This Tunisian-inspired technique produces great color art that is impossible to achieve with other types of crochet.

Items you can make with the crochet hook technique

- hand towels
- Shawls
- Baby throws

6.11 Crochet fillet

Chains and double crochet were used to make this crochet pattern. That's a grid-like design where spaces have been either filled or left empty, as well as the piece's pictures are made from the empty spaces. The specialty of fillet crochet is that both filled & vacant squares of such cloth can be used to embed images.

Things you can do using fillet crochet

- Baby throws
- Kimonos and jackets
- Handbags
- Pillows

6.12 Hand crocheting

Finger crochet is quite comparable to finger knitting in that it is the same as crocheting, having a hook absent. In essence, it is a type of crochet-inspired hand cloth weaving. Starting with finger crochet is enjoyable, but since the resulting tension is very loose, you'll definitely want to switch to using a hook pretty fast and create more adaptable designs.

Items you can create with finger crochet

- Easy-to-use string bags
- Simple scarves

6.13 Freeform crochet

This type of crochet is made without the use of a pattern or established strategy. It is a very natural and creative style of crochet. It should be noted that if you're a control freak (like us), this may not be your cup of tea. If you suffer like i do without direction or a plan, stay away from freeform.

Items you may create using freeform crochet

- Times for one-off apparel
- Works of art

6.14 Crochet with hairpins

While using a regular crochets hook and holding the crocheted fabric taut across two thin metal rods, this technique is comparable to broomstick crochet. This method's name derives from the fact that metal hairpins were utilized when it was first developed. This design produces an incredibly distinctive finished cloth.

Items you can make with hairpin crochet

- Pretty scarves

The shawls

- wraps

6.15 Miniature crochet

A really fine thread & very few crochet hooks are used to create this modern form of crochet. This delicate task is perhaps better suited for crocheters with greater patience.

Things you can make utilizing micro crochet

- Very small things
- Accentuations
- Tasman

6.16 Crochet overlay

A method in which stitches are placed on top of a foundation of crochet to produce a raised pattern. This provides numerous opportunities for stunning and detailed color work.

Items you can create with overlay crochet

- Pot restraints
- Wall décor
- Handbags

6.17 Crochet pineapple

This is more of a broad stitch and form pattern than it is really a technique. Pineapples can be used to crochet doilies, scarves, and even clothes. Once you learn to recognize the crochet pineapple, you begin to see them all around. This stitch pattern gained popularity in the 1970s.

Items you can create with pineapple crochet

- Clothes
- tops

The shawls

- wraps

6.18 Crocheted stained glass

Very reminiscent of overlay crochet, although usually accomplished using black yarn to give the appearance of stained glass. A distinctive and eye-catching crochet design.

Crafts you may create with crochet in the style of stained glass

- Heavy, durable things
- Scarves for winter
- Purses

6.19 Crochet symbols

This is frequently featured in Japanese crochet books and is also referred to as chart crochet. It's a really important ability to master since you may use the charts in just about any sign crochet book, written in any language, to complete the projects. Remember: once you master crocheting from symbol patterns, your entire life will change.

Items you may construct with the crochet symbol style

- Complex patterns which are challenging to explain verbally
- Complex designs
- Themes
- Phraseology of other languages

6.20 Crocheted tapestries

This is similar to color work in crochet. Intarsia crochet is another name for it. In tapestry crochet, a variety of various ways to work, and each way produces a different end product. One of the numerous methods to accomplish color work in crochet is through tapestries.

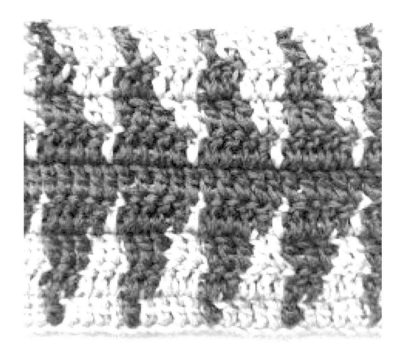

Items you may create with tapestry crochet

- Colorful artwork
- Designs based on imagery

6.21 Tunisian crochet

Tunisian crochet seems nearly identical to knitting, in which you have several active loops anywhere at a particular time & you work the loops on & off your hook, exactly like in knitting. Tunisian crochet is performed on a lengthy hook with such a brake at the base or a hook with such a cord connection.

Things you can create with Tunisian crochet

Knit-style clothing

- Coverlets
- Shawls

Chapter 7

Common beginning crochet errors to prevent

7.1 Beginning a project with the incorrect link in the chain

The initial chain from the hook is essentially the last actually finished chain you made because you do not even count the initial chain on the hook. View the image below. Wouldn't count your loop on the hook; instead, count the very first chain, which is entirely made; the next chain is the subsequent loop from your hook; and so forth.

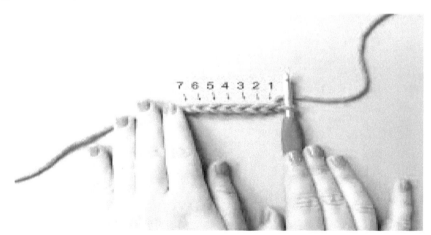

7.2 Using linked chains as starting loops rather than a magic loop

Starting a crochet project in the round can be done in one of two ways. One is to create four or five chains & slip stitch them together into a circle. Most novices are instructed to create

granny squares in this manner. A magic circle is a good place to start because it is cleaner and more flexible. The center of the magic circle is more compact than that of your chain link circle, as can be seen in the photograph. The majority of the time, this comes down to personal preference; however, when knitting in the round, we almost frequently employ a magic circle. The key is to maintain consistency. Choose either the rope link or the magic circle as the main motif for the project if it is based on a theme.

7.3 Make the chain utilizing the same length hook as the remainder of your item.

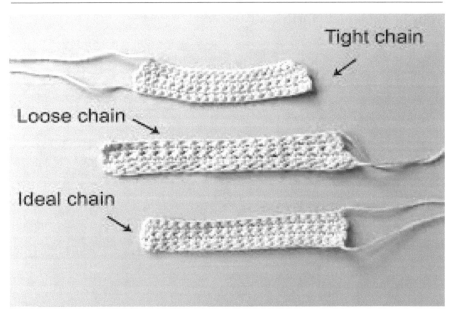

Did you ever begin a project only to realize that something is slightly off? The problem is most frequently (knot), in which your beginning chain is just too tight. This is especially typical

among novice crocheters. The graphic below illustrates how crucial it is to obtain the proper chain tension in order to avoid having your project ruined. The best way to acquire the proper stress for the chain is to employ a relatively greater loop than the design calls for. If the chain tension is fine, you can use the exact size hook, but if the foundation row is buckling because the chain is too tight, move up a hook size.

7.4 Crochet that gets bigger or smaller

If you're able to see the project slowly expanding or contracting, something is wrong. You're most likely placing your initial stitch in the incorrect location.

In mono crochet, the very first stitch you make is inserted into the initial thread of the row before it.

Your turning chain serves as the initial stitch for the remaining basic stitches; therefore, you're true first stitch moves into your second stitch of such a row before.

7.5 Adhering to the manufacturer's knots

Sad to say, any ball of yarn that you purchase is almost certainly going to have a minimum of 1 knot in it. This knot is not reliable. The best course of action is to take the knot apart and use a Russian joint to reattach it.

7.6 Not being taught how to "see" the stitches.

The majority of novice crocheters are too preoccupied attempting to yarn through their hook to truly pay attention to the appearance of the stitch as they make it. This is completely comprehensible. Like training to drive a vehicle, practicing crochet is similar.

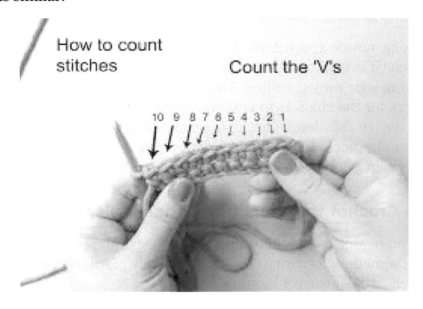

There are numerous moving pieces, and finding your groove takes time. Take some time when you first begin crocheting to count the stitches & become familiar with their appearance.

7.7 Refusing to learn new skills because they seem difficult

Edie Ekman, who taught me how to crochet, claims that all crocheting entails is dragging yarn thru a variety of loop configurations. Most patterns can be finished if you know how

to single crochet, doubling crochet, treble crochet, loop, & slip stitch, in fact. Some of the most complex designs are composed of variations on the fundamental stitches. Just try it out if you notice a project you want to develop. There is no reason that you shouldn't succeed if you spend some time, adhere to the pattern, & read extremely carefully.

7.8 Lack of knowledge of high-quality yarn

We'll be honest: we have slight yarn snobbery. We enjoy working with natural fibers because we enjoy the stitch quality; we work with 100% cotton around 80% of the time. Although we don't have anything against the cheap yarn, we discovered that low-quality acrylics wouldn't drape well or, worse, scream and feel hard in my palm as we crochet. You can get my shopping guide for yarn as well. It helps beginners feel much less anxious about their trips to the yarn store.

7.9 Ignoring the fact that the flipping chain is equal to the width of the initial row's stitch

The opening chain at the outset of a row raises the length to whatever pattern you intend to make during that row, though i don't like to say how long it required us to realize this. Then, sc is one chain; hdc is two chains, and so on. Don't you think that makes complete sense at this point?

7.10 Failing to learn c2c

It's an extremely simple and fast way to make a blanket. Although it initially sounds challenging, it is actually rather simple when you get the feel of it. For novices, this project is quite rewarding.

This c2c baby blanket design is a great way to learn how to crochet in corners, as well as the hub includes detailed directions for making both rectangle & square blankets.

7.11 Ignoring the circular crochet technique

Although beginning to crochet a round initially looks intimidating, once you grasp the principals involved, you'll be crocheting items each round like such a total boss. T-shirt yarn

hampers are a fantastic place to begin if you've not worked in a circular fashion before. You can clearly understand what you're doing because the stitches are large and clearly defined.

7.12 Failing to properly weave in ends

The greatest rookie mistake is this. We had believed that you simply twisted them like you'd do if you had been sewing when you initially started crocheting. As you finish a job, it's crucial to properly weave your ends in. I am aware that many crocheters despise the ends, but they are necessary for the process.

7.13 Focusing on minor errors

Whatever you make when you initially start out won't look all that spectacular. That's completely ok. Get some cheap yarn and start hooking? Try new things and make errors. We can crochet quite well today, but remember when we first started? We failed. Don't worry if you miss a stitch—just reverse it and continue if it doesn't bother you. That is the appeal of home-made goods. It has lovely flaws and a lot of personalities.

7.14 Resigning too soon

Nothing saddens me even more as a crochet instructor than to witness a student give up without giving it their all. Too many individuals mistakenly believe that all it takes to create wonderful creations is the use of a hook, yet this ability requires

practice and patience. During the first few, you'll seem like you're composed of thumbs and fingers, but eventually, everything will click into place, or you'll find yourself crocheting without even realizing it. Getting to the point that you can crochet while watching TV or talking to friends is worthwhile. Then you can continue to crochet continuously.

Chapter 8
Blocking the crochet

Three techniques for blocking crochet

Why do you block crops?

Many good things happen to the crochet work as a result of blocking.

The stitches become more open, less wrinkled, & drapery as a result.

Another benefit of blocking crochet is that it gives the creations a polished appearance.

Steps for beginning to block the crochet

Hopefully, the aforementioned examples have helped you understand the enormous impact blocking may make.

When blocking has become so advantageous, how do you do it?

Step one is to not be terrified. Seriously, if you approach blocking like a terrifying monster, you'll never begin doing it.

It isn't as difficult as you may imagine, so believe us. We almost can't believe we are saying this, but we now look forward to blocking. It has turned into a crocheting phase that we eagerly anticipate, & it may be the same for you. To find out how to limit your own projects, keep reading.

We'll demonstrate three simple techniques for you & go through each one in detail.

Crochet blocking boards/mats

You might be thinking, "Now, do we really need a blocking mat?"

Even though various materials are used for each blocking technique, all of them could profit from possessing a blocking mat.

However, using such a blocking board and mat will be much simpler if you have one (they work the same way).

What you will need

Blocking with wet, spray, & steam

Let me briefly summarise the three approaches you can utilize before we go into blocking. Wet blocking is the term for the first one. Personally, we think this is the best approach. All natural fibers can be used with it, & it will guarantee that your creation can stretch completely and keep its shape after use.

The following technique is called spray blocking. Spray blocking is ideal for minor applications that require blocking but do not require significant stretching. Again, natural fibers respond well to this technique.

Blocking your steam is the final approach. We were most hesitant to try this one, yet it's not as difficult as we had anticipated. Acrylic yarn may be steam blocked, and it will

completely change your crocheting experience. We mean it. We were genuinely astonished by how effectively the steam-blocking cowl that we showed you in the images performed.

So stop waiting now. Let's explore these techniques together.

8.1 Method 1: Wet blocking

Use this technique if

Any natural fiber is used in your project.

You are working on a project which requires a lot of stretching or shaping.

If your creation is composed of acrylic yarn, don't use this procedure. Acrylic is unaffected by dampness, unlike natural fibers.

Materials:

A sink

2 linens

Pins

Step 1:

Add cold or moderate water to the sink. You should not allow the water should become hot when you're utilizing natural fibers for wet blocking. (Except, of course, if you intend to felt it—in which case, blocking would be the reverse)

Step 2:

Put the project completely submerged in water.

Step 3:

Your project should soak. It should be left to sit once completely saturated. We usually leave ours for 15 to 20 minutes. To make sure everything is sufficiently moist, you might wish to turn in a large project midway through.

Step 4:

Shut off the sink. Thoroughly squeeze all water out of your craft.

When you compress it, do not bend it since this may lead it to change shape. Instead, take substantial portions & press the water out with your hands. Keep in mind that this method won't completely drain the water. That's the purpose of the next action is for.

Step 5:

Roll the project in something like a towel and hold it there. To absorb any extra water, gently press the towel down all over.

Step 6:

Place a second towel flat on the ground. Lay out your crocheted item on it. If you'd like, you might consider using a blocking board throughout the place of the towel, although in our experience, a towel works just well.

Step 7:

On the towel, tack your project. When you're completed, place the stitches precisely as you want them to. Wet blocking is all about stretching the cloth to its maximum extent, so don't be scared to do it.

Step 8:

Your project has to dry completely. To make sure it is completely dry, we usually let it lie overnight. You're finished after you remove the pins, of course.

8.2 Method 2: Blocking spray

Apply this method when:

Your work is constructed using natural fibers.

There is no need to dramatically extend your project.

You have a little period of time to do the blocking.

If the project requires a lot of shaping and stretching, avoid using this method. Utilize wet blocking for that kind of project instead.

Materials:

Pins

Towel

Aerosol can

Step 1:

Your project should be spread across a towel or blocking board and nailed down.

Step 2:

Spray the project with water till it is moist with a plastic container. (Use wet blocking rather than spray blocking if the project requires to be completely submerged in water to block & stretch properly.)

Step 3:

Remove pins when your project has had time to dry. All matters, in the end, are that.

8.3 Steam blocking method

Apply this method when:

You used acrylic yarn to make your craft.

Your project must be greatly stretched.

Materials:

Pins (optional)

Blocking board or a towel

Use a steaming setting on an iron

Step 1:

Your project should be spread across a cloth as well as a

blocking board. You should secure it if it wants to be extended out significantly, such as the lace cowl we displayed at the start. Pinning isn't required for all items, especially those that aren't laced.

Step 2:

Get your iron ready. Put it to "steam," add water, and wait for it to warm up.

Step 3:

Place the iron directly over the project. Never contact the ironing to the crocheted piece; otherwise, it will melt. This really is due to the fact that acrylic yarn is basically composed of plastic. Making this is known as "killing" the project. You must still hold your iron at a minimum of one inch above the project, though. You'll be good as long even as iron never comes into contact with the yarn directly. You may approach the project as closely as you like but exercise caution.

Step 4:

Don't be afraid to use the steam, merely allow it to run until your product has a little mist on it. After that, take the pins out.

There you have it, the three blocking techniques. Not that difficult, are we right? Each technique will always get simpler and simpler as you use it. You just might come to like it.

Let's discuss a few more frequently asked topics about blocking while we wrap up.

Chapter 9
21 Frequently asked crochet questions

We've mostly been compelled to spend plenty of time indoors since the beginning of 2020. Despite the fact that it's quite challenging, the additional indoor leisure has led to many of us turning to create as a way to decompress. And the ensuing crafting explosion has made thousands of people happy in their residences and online. Another of the crafts which took off during the epidemic was crochet. It is not too late whether you've thought of taking up this fantastic activity. Here are 21 frequently asked questions to assist you in determining if it's the correct option for you.

9.1 How can I learn crochet the best?

You might choose a book & try to learn the stitches & patterns in it. But seeing anyone else crochet seems to be the greatest way to learn how to do it yourself. You can perform the crocheting motions without opening your eyes if you have assimilated them to that stage through the multimedia learning component.

9.2 What are the differences between knitting & crochet?

The fundamental distinction between knitting & crochet is the equipment. In contrast to crochet, knitting simply needs a

single hook. The varied stitches used in the 2 crafts also give the finished products different faces; knit items have more elasticity and drape, whilst crochet pieces are firmer and retain their shape better.

Both knitting & crochet can be used to create the same kinds of goods, from warm blankets to accessories like scarves & sweaters. Whatever type of yarn will work for both projects.

9.3 Is knitting difficult?

It's not difficult to crochet. There will be a period of adjustment when you first start, just like with any craft. You'll need to practice grasping the hook, working with the yarn, & understanding a pattern. These abilities will come easier with time and practice.

9.4 What is crochet's history?

In the 19th century, contemporary crochet gained popularity in Europe. Tambouring, a term coined from traditional Middle Eastern needlework skills, was its ancestor. In this ancient technique, loop stitching was done over a foundation fabric. The backdrop fabric was eventually taken off, but the stitching remained.

In the 18th century, French craftsman riego de la branchardiere created millions of crochet patterns using lace designs. Additionally, poor employees made garments out of crochet

during the Irish potato famine, which enabled them to survive. The skill gained popularity and grew into a mainstay after a wave of Irish immigrants arrived in the United States.

9.5 Is knitting easier than crochet?

Really, it all entails the individual as well as the undertaking. Knitting frequently tests your hand coordination because it uses two needles. Additionally, dropping a stitch during knitting can completely sabotage your product.

However, a lot of individuals believe that learning to knit is originally simpler than learning to crochet. Additionally, knitting is significantly better suited to producing garments because its chunkier stitches are typically stiffer than knitting stitches. Each craft actually has advantages and disadvantages.

9.6 Who created crochet?

The invention of crochet cannot be attributed to a single person. The origins are disputed by historians; some place them in 1500s Italy, while others place them in ancient times or possibly South America. Whatever its origins, the fact remains that crochet developed from a variety of crafts, including knitting, embroidery, & tapestry, and it's still evolving today.

9.7 When was that crochet first created?

Again, it is challenging to determine a precise date. Despite not being mentioned till the 19th century, contemporary crochet appears to have its roots in the European tradition. However, older arts that require comparable skills have made a significant contribution to the crochet people know today. Comparable crocheting methods can be found in Middle Eastern needlework, Chinese 3-dimensional woven dolls, & South American ceremonial adornments, all of which date back centuries before modern crochet.

9.8 What crafts can anyone crochet?

Amigurumi bees

Amigurumi, which is a Japanese craft, is used to create adorable objects such as these bumblebees.

You may crochet anything you see. Although the technique is typically used to produce blankets, caps, or scarves, one may make whatever one wishes with it. The possibilities are endless: sweaters, mittens, washcloths, placemats, affiliate dolls, toilet seat cushions, etc. Even if you might not be able to get the ideal dog sweater design, you can create your personality with a little perseverance.

9.9 Is crochet simple to do?

Absolutely. The crochet hook, thread, as well as a set of scissors is the only tools needed to make a crochet project. You may start crocheting a project in a matter of hours if you're able to learn a few fundamental methods & one or 2 basic stitches.

Additionally, it is quite simple to expand on the fundamentals and produce more sophisticated applications when you have these down. With every project you finish, your crocheting abilities will drastically improve.

9.10 Which is faster, knitting or crocheting?

Generally speaking, crochet is quicker, but it also differs depending on the individual as well as the project. Creating something intricate like a sweater with crocheting can take a very long time and will test your patience greatly. It also takes more time to build up sewing stitches because they are often smaller compared to crochet ones.

However, compared to knitting crafts, crochet projects typically utilize more yarn. Therefore, complex projects involving a large amount of yarn may require more time than a knitted project of similar complexity.

9.11 How many stitches are there in crochet?

There are more than a hundred distinct crochet stitches. The majority, however, are permutations of the fall stitch, solitary, half double, as well as double stitches.

There will always be at most a single of these stitches included in a pattern. And they produce a wide variety of aesthetics when combined in various ways. All stitches, including popcorns, picots, and puffs, will use one of the fundamental four.

9.12 Does crocheting benefit the brain?

Crocheting has a lot of advantages for the mind. Studies have revealed that regular, repetitive actions significantly increase your serotonin levels. It's also been connected to a lower risk of dementia.

It has been shown that mastering a new ability makes your brain develop new synapses, which facilitates future learning. Nothing compares to the pride & happiness you feel when you grasp your finished crochet masterpiece in your hands.

9.13 How much does crocheting cost?

The cost of crochet is relatively low. A skein of yarn or one tool is all you need. These 2 alone will cost you about $5 to create a scarf or cap.

Of course, you'll require extra yarn if your project is larger. However, your neighborhood craft store has so much high-

quality yarn that it should never be difficult for you to discover affordable alternatives. If you develop the "yarn bug," an obsession with purchasing quite so many skeins that there are colors in the spectrum, it simply becomes pricey.

9.14 Is knitting beneficial for arthritis?

According to studies, when done correctly, it can lessen the effects of arthritis complaints. Crafts requiring needlework, such as crocheting, can strengthen and texturize the hands.

Stretching and taking breaks are beneficial when engaging in any repetitive activity. Additionally, there are comfortable hooks featuring handles that reduce hand fatigue. Above all, seek a professional opinion from your physician if you have concerns about arthritis.

9.15 Can I learn to crochet on my own?

The majority of individuals believe that visual learning provides the most effective. Written directions are frequently fairly dull and could be difficult to understand. The quickest path to success is to observe a pro and follow along with them because they crochet.

9.16 Is crochet an art form?

Art and craft have always been in conflict with one another. Both need a great deal of expertise, but art frequently stands out because it's viewed as a method of a self-artist "expressing"

something via their work. This classification would typically place it in the handicraft column.

Nevertheless, as crochet develops, there are countless more ways for a crocheter can represent themselves through their creations. There are methods for using yarn to make significant, moving visuals. There are tactile, 3-dimensional vistas that rival any van gogh picture in beauty. The user can even make delicate features that seem to be finer than that of a painter's brush with thread crochet.

Suppose you discover that this is their preferred medium and that you have things to say; congratulations. You're a creator.

9.17 When learning to crochet, what else should i learn first?

The greatest starting point if you're a beginner is to educate yourself on the necessary tools. It is crucial to understand the many types of hooks and how to grasp them since they'll be your best friends.

You should then learn how to make a chain along with the most fundamental stitch, the solitary crochet. You can still create a bedspread big sufficient for a California big bed if that is the sole stitch you learn.

9.18 Can crochet help you relax?

It might be really calming. Numerous studies have demonstrated how repetitive activities, such as crocheting, can reduce heart rate, increase serotonin, and promote relaxation on par with yoga or meditation. You'll enter into crafting ecstasy if you pair it up with a beverage of choice, and your go-to binge-watch show—great British bake-off, is strongly suggested.

9.19 Is crocheting enjoyable?

It is a lot of fun. It gives you the delight of crafting anything with your hands while letting you express your creativity via colors and textures. Giving a colleague or a beloved one a special gift which you spent countless hours making with care and attention also brings about a great deal of satisfaction. This is indeed a craft that never goes out of style.

9.20 Is crochet regaining popularity?

Definitely, a similar-sized boom like the one in the 1960s & 1970s is currently occurring in the craft industry. Beginning in 2022, target will start stocking crochet jerseys on its racks, joining the trend. It's an excellent idea to pick up a claw right now more than before.

9.21 Which yarn should i utilize for crochet?

Yarn is available in a plethora of designs and hues. When selecting yarn, fiber type & weight are the 2 key factors you should take into account.

All types of fiber, including cotton, cashmere, silk, acrylic, nylon & other synthetic mixtures, are used to make yarn. Cotton works well for socks, whereas synthetic yarns work well for huge blankets. Different fibers are better suited for different jobs.

The weight of a yarn describes how thick it is. Your stitches will be larger the stronger the yarn is. The recommended yarn weight for your work will be provided by design.

Conclusion

You can begin creating your crochet crafts after possessing all the essential materials. It brings such joy to crochet. You'll adore the concept of making complex patterns using only a hook as well as yarn. Consider the opportunities. Having said that, daily use of these crocheting tools will significantly improve your ability and toolkit.

These many crochet stitches serve as the building blocks for creative crocheting. If you are familiar with the fundamental crochet stitches, you can finish these quickly.

We implore you to attempt the stitch that scares you the most.

That is how we advance.

Despite the fact that these are merely the most fundamental crochet stitches for amateurs, you may create a wide variety of items with them. If you enjoy amigurumi, single crochet is used to create adorable small plush creatures.

These fundamental stitches can be used to create a scarf, gardening gloves, mittens, as well as a cozy baby blanket. Try it out, hone your abilities, and eventually, you'll be able to make that stunning long red scarf that is impossible to buy elsewhere in the shops. It is really simple to become "hooked" on this activity.

Since everyone must start somewhere & practice makes complete, you wouldn't need to be an expert to start.

Any beginner will find these quick & simple crochet patterns to be the ideal place to start. They'll aid you in honing your crocheting abilities as well. Cast on while you rest and recline. It's time to enjoy crocheting's calming effects.

After you've mastered a few simple stitch projects, such as crocheting scarves, washcloths, an infinity scarf, or a cowl, we would advise storing items like socks, snowmen, as well as other crochet initiatives with a bit of texture & form. Expand your repertoire to include items that require some shaping, such as a crocheted hat, a shawl with trying to shape, or a simple slipper pattern. As you gain experience, try increasingly challenging patterns.

Made in United States
Troutdale, OR
07/15/2023

11290605R00066